D1717024

KNOWLEDGE ENCYCLOPEDIA

STARS AND GALAXIES
SPACE

(An imprint of Prakash Books Pvt. Ltd.)

Wonder House Books
Corporate & Editorial Office
113-A, 1st Floor, Ansari Road, Daryaganj, New Delhi-110002
Tel +91 11 2324 7062-65

Disclaimer: The information contained in this encyclopedia has been collated with inputs from subject experts. All information contained herein is true to the best of the Publisher's knowledge.

Printed in 2020 in India

ISBN : 9789390391349

Table of Contents

THE AMAZING WORLD OF STARS

Some of the brightest celestial objects that light up our night skies are the infinite and shining stars. They have fascinated human beings since time immemorial and have played an important role in navigation and the study of our mysterious universe.

How many of these huge luminous balls of gas, composed mainly of hydrogen and helium, exist in the universe? Are they scattered randomly in space, or are they clustered together in dense groups? Besides the Sun, are the other stars really light years away?

The study of stars helps scientists understand the evolution of galaxies and life itself! So, studying them and their life cycles is critical and central to the field of astronomy.

▼ Stargazing means to observe the stars in the night sky with or without a telescope

Starstruck

Stars are the main building blocks of a galaxy. Astronomers and scientists have been studying stars for many centuries. By studying the age, distribution and composition of stars in a galaxy, scientists are able to glean important information regarding the history and evolution of that galaxy. Most of the stars that are observable from Earth lie in our Milky Way galaxy or in the Andromeda galaxy—a major galaxy closest to the Milky Way.

 ## How I Wonder What You Are?

A star is a massive **self-luminous** ball made up of very hot gases (mostly hydrogen and helium). Stars shine and release energy by burning hydrogen into helium at their cores through a process known as **nuclear fusion**. Outside the core, energy is released outwards by a process called **radiation**. Closer to the surface, energy moves out by **convection** where hot gases rise, cool down and then sink back to the surface.

All stars are not the same, they vary in appearance, size, mass, colour, temperature, etc. Stars exist either alone, such as the Sun, or they exist in pairs or clusters. All the countless stars which are viewed in the galaxies are generally studied and observed in comparison to the Sun.

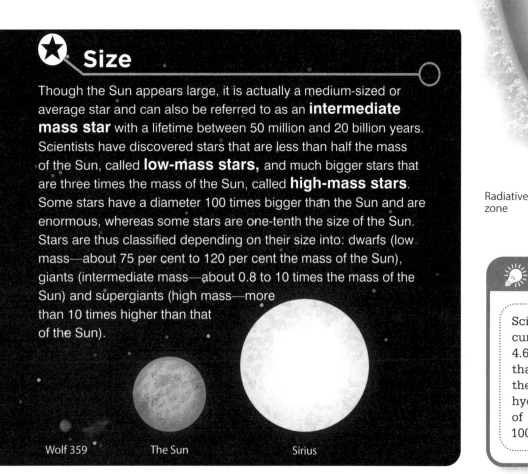

Photosphere (6,500–4,000 K)

▼ *This photograph of the Sun shows nuclear fusion at its core, radiation outside the core and convection on the surface*

Core

Radiative zone

Size

Though the Sun appears large, it is actually a medium-sized or average star and can also be referred to as an **intermediate mass star** with a lifetime between 50 million and 20 billion years. Scientists have discovered stars that are less than half the mass of the Sun, called **low-mass stars,** and much bigger stars that are three times the mass of the Sun, called **high-mass stars**. Some stars have a diameter 100 times bigger than the Sun and are enormous, whereas some stars are one-tenth the size of the Sun. Stars are thus classified depending on their size into: dwarfs (low mass—about 75 per cent to 120 per cent the mass of the Sun), giants (intermediate mass—about 0.8 to 10 times the mass of the Sun) and supergiants (high mass—more than 10 times higher than that of the Sun).

Wolf 359   The Sun   Sirius

 ## Isn't It Amazing!

Scientists believe that the current age of the Sun is around 4.6 billion years. They believe that after 4.6 billion more years, the Sun will have used up all of its hydrogen fuel and the temperature of its core will increase by 100 million degrees!

⭐ Colour

All stars are hot, but they vary in the degree of their hotness. The temperature of stars determines their colour or appearance. The hottest stars appear white or blue. Stars with an orange or yellow hue are cooler in comparison and red stars are cooler still. Our Sun is classified as a yellow star on this spectrum.

Convection zone

3000 K 4000 K 6000 K 7000 K 10,000 K 20,000 K 30,000 K

Coldest ⟶ Hottest

▲ *Blue stars are the hottest, compared to the red and orange stars, which are cooler (K = Kelvin)*

Flare

⭐ Shining Bright

The brightness of a star depends on **luminosity**, which is the amount of light emitted by an object in a unit of time. Luminosity depends on the radius of the star, its surface temperature and its distance from Earth. Scientists use a luminosity scale of grades to distinguish stars. According to the luminosity scale, grade I is for supergiants, grade II for bright giants, grade III for normal giants, grade IV for subgiants and grade V for main sequence or dwarf stars.

▲ *A luminous star*

👤 In Real Life

In 2011, scientists discovered a brown dwarf star (CFBDSIR 1458 10b) and found that it was the same temperature as a freshly made cup of coffee! At a distance of 75 **light years**, with a surface temperature of 97° C, it is the coldest brown dwarf seen since then. It was also noted to be a failed star since it had heat and chemical properties like regular stars, but not enough mass for nuclear fusion at its centre.

⭐ Hot, Hot Star

Astronomers since the 1860s have classified stars and put them in an order depending on their surface temperature. The scheme of ordering stars this way is referred to as a **stellar classification.** For example, the Sun is a yellow dwarf star with a surface temperature of about 5,500° C and is designated as G2 V, with G2 standing for the second hottest star of the yellow G class and the V representing the luminosity grade of a main sequence or dwarf star.

The Science Behind Stars

There are trillions of stars in the sky. These stars are massive in size and are made up of extremely hot gases. They have a long lifespan and do not burn up until after millions or billions of years in a slow process of evolution. They begin to burn up after all their fuel is used up. A star like our Sun would have a lifespan of about 10 billion years. But what scientific principles keep a star together and can we really know how many stars exist in our universe?

 ## Staying Intact

Stars produce tonnes of energy by burning a large amount of nuclear fuel within their cores. Have you ever wondered then, how such hot objects continue to shine for billions of years without exploding? Heat from the nuclear fuel burning in the star's core generates outward-moving pressure. On the other hand, each star's gravity exerts an inward force, trying to squeeze it into a small, tight ball. Therefore, a star is kept intact due to these two opposing forces.

A neutron star can remain intact even under rapid rotation. It does not break apart. Even a **black hole** would remain intact under such rotation, but it would not send any signal. 'Dead' stars are those that have used up all of their nuclear fuels. Sometimes they can actually produce more energy when they are dead than they did when they were 'alive'.

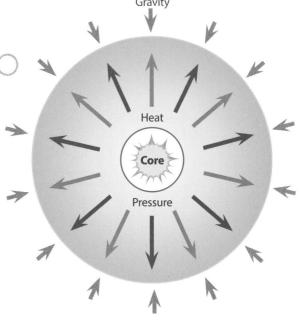

▲ *Opposing forces of pressure and gravity prevent a star from collapsing*

 ## Stars Galore

Although there are trillions of stars in the observable universe, only a fraction of these are visible to the naked eye and we can never really count the number of stars that exist. On a clear and dark night, we can probably see only 3,000 stars without the use of a telescope.

In fact, our universe is so vast and expansive that it has more than 100 billion galaxies and each of these galaxies is most likely to have more than 100 billion stars!

▲ *Although there are an infinite number of stars in the universe, we can only view a few thousand without a telescope*

In Real Life

Stargazing is an exciting and interesting hobby that can be taken up by anyone who wants to learn more about the stars. One does not necessarily need binoculars or a telescope (though these would help) to admire celestial objects or to view astronomical phenomena. A star atlas is also a handy tool.

Some stars can be seen by the naked eye. Once you get familiar with the star patterns or **constellations**, you can easily identify them. Well-known constellations like Orion the Hunter or the Little Dipper are a few such star formations. If you are lucky, you may even be able to see the Andromeda galaxy—the most distant celestial object which can be seen by the unaided eye!

Ornaments in the Sky

Stars are so far away from Earth that they appear like tiny, shining diamonds in the night sky. But do stars really twinkle? Do planets twinkle? Why can we not see stars during the day?

Twinkle, Twinkle Little Star

Despite what the popular children's poem says, stars do not actually twinkle. Stars are located at such great distances that, even from a telescope, they appear as pinpoints of light in the night. Since all the light from a star comes from a single point, it only appears to twinkle when seen from Earth due to the effects of our planet's atmosphere. Atmospheric winds and differences in temperatures and densities affect starlight when it enters our atmosphere, causing the light from the star to twinkle when seen from the surface of Earth.

▲ The Hubble telescope has managed to get clear images of stars because there is no atmosphere in space

Do Planets Twinkle?

Planets are closer to Earth than stars. When seen from a telescope, stars look like pinpoints, but planets appear as tiny discs. The light from planets is also distorted by Earth's atmosphere as it travels toward our eyes. But while the light from one edge of a planet may travel one way, the light from the opposite edge of the planet might go in the opposite direction. This refraction (slight change in direction) of light from different edges of a planet is such that planets appear to shine steadily. They do not twinkle.

▲ Planets appear to shine steadily, they do not twinkle like stars

Morning Sky

The gases and particles present in the atmosphere scatter sunlight in all directions. Blue light travels as shorter and smaller waves and is scattered more than the other colours. Blue light is much brighter than the dim light coming from the stars, and hence we cannot see the stars even though they are still glowing. If you were on the Moon, however, you would be able to see the stars all the time since the Moon does not have any atmosphere to distort the light originating from the stars.

▼ Stars cannot be viewed during the day due to the intense glare of the Sun

💡 Isn't It Amazing!

Did you know that stars in the sky 'make music' and they never stop playing this celestial concert? Stars have an umpteen number of different sound waves or different 'notes' bouncing around inside them. Bigger stars make more low and deep sounds like a double bass, whereas smaller stars have more high-pitched tunes, like flutes. Unfortunately, you cannot hear this music with your ears; scientists are able to listen to these harmonies or sound waves using very powerful and sensitive telescopes. With these, they are able to understand what stars are made of, their size and age and how they contribute to the evolution of the Milky Way galaxy. NASA's Kepler space telescope, which has now run out of fuel, and NASA's Transiting Exoplanet Survey Satellite (TESS) are two such pieces of equipment that can detect these stellar sound waves and vibrations.

Star Systems and Clusters

Galaxies are home to the stars. The Milky Way and the Andromeda galaxy consist of millions of them. Generally, stars exist in the universe either in pairs called a **binary system** or in clusters. Some stars, like the Sun, exist alone.

Binary Star System

A binary system is when two stars are bound together by gravitational forces and orbit around a common centre of mass. A large number of stars, perhaps one-half of all stars in the Milky Way galaxy, are either binaries or part of a complex multiple system.

▲ *A binary star system contains two stars and is a very common occurrence in the universe*

Incredible Individuals

Friedrich von Struve (1793–1864) was born in Germany but fled his country in 1808 in order to avoid getting enlisted for war by Napoleon's army. He first went to Denmark and later to Russia, which is where he spent most of his life. He is one of the great astronomers of the 19th century and the first generation of accomplished astronomers in his family.

He established and pioneered the study of binary stars. In 1824, he acquired a telescope which was far more advanced in technology than anything seen before. He used it for his unmatched survey of binary stars. In fact, he surveyed 1,20,000 stars in the Northern Hemisphere and measured 3,112 binaries, more than 75 per cent of which were still unknown at that time. His catalogue on binary-star astronomy, published in 1837, is a well-known classic.

Star Clusters

Star clusters are mainly classified into **open** and **globular clusters**. A star cluster is bound together by the mutual gravitational pull of its members and is physically related through common origin.

The year 1847 marked the beginning of the study of star clusters in external galaxies. It was started by Sir John William Herschel at the Cape Observatory in South Africa. He published a list of these clusters found in the Magellanic Clouds, the **dwarf galaxies** orbiting the Milky Way galaxy. In the 20th century, with the help of a large reflector and specialised equipment like the Schmidt telescopes, it was possible to extend this study and identify such clusters in more remote galaxies.

▼ *Star clusters seen in the Milky Way galaxy*

⭐ Open Clusters

They are groups of young stars, usually containing a dozen or many hundred stars. They are generally found in asymmetrical arrangements.

The Pleiades and Hyades in the constellation of Taurus; Praesepe (the Beehive) in the constellation of Cancer and Coma Berenices ('Berenice's Hair' in Latin) are four such **open clusters** known to us from the earliest times. The Pleiades has historic significance since people from some early cultures determined the start of their year with the rising of this cluster.

▲ *The open star cluster of Pleiades is also called Seven Sisters or Messier 45*

💡 Isn't It Amazing!

For centuries, astronomers and space lovers have hungered to see and understand the mysteries of the universe. The Hubble Telescope launched by NASA in 1990, helped astronomers achieve this goal. Hubble orbits Earth and since it is situated above our atmosphere, it is able to get a bird's eye view of the universe and send back thousands of useful images to Earth, without the distortions that would otherwise be seen if viewed from a telescope on the ground.

Hubble, which is nearly the size of a large school bus, is one of NASA's most successful and longest lasting missions. The photographs sent by Hubble have been vital in answering many questions that astronomers have had and continue to have about the universe.

◀ *A model of the 3D Hubble Space Telescope*

▲ *The Seagull nebula with open clusters and globular clusters of stars*

⭐ Globular Clusters

These, on the other hand, comprise older star systems containing hundreds of thousands of stars which are closely packed in a symmetrical, roughly spherical form.

Omega Centauri and Messier 13 in the constellation of Hercules are two examples of globular clusters visible to the naked eye as fuzzy patches of light. By the early years of the 21st century, over 150 globular clusters were discovered in the Milky Way galaxy. The study of open and globular clusters helped scientists understand the Milky Way galaxy.

⭐ Associations

These are other groups of stars which are also recognised and are made up of a few dozen to hundreds of stars of similar type and common origin whose density is less than that of the surrounding field. Knowledge of the characteristics and motions of individual stars dispersed over a large area helped scientists in the discovery of stellar associations. In the 1920s, it was found that young, hot blue stars apparently grouped together. A Soviet astronomer, Victor Ambartsumian, suggested in 1949 that these stars are members of physical groupings of stars with a common origin.

The Birth of a Star

Like animals and human beings, stars are also born and they die. However, stars live for and evolve over billions of years. If all of us lived for billions of years, like stars do, we would need numerous Earth-like planets to fit everyone in! Luckily, our universe has no such 'space' problems and although it is constantly growing and expanding, it is so vast that it can contain billions and trillions of celestial objects and systems including stars, planets and galaxies.

 ## A Stellar Journey

▼ Space is colourful. It contains many examples of colourful, nebulous stars and galaxies

The journey of a star is intriguing! Just like human beings go through major life stages like childhood, adolescence and so on, the life cycle of a star also starts from birth, until it attains maturity and then finally dies.
A star matures differently depending upon its size and the matter it contains. The larger the mass of a star, the shorter its lifespan.

 ## The Beginning

Stars are born in the universe in a cloud of gas (consisting mostly of hydrogen and helium) and dust known as a **nebula**. Later, stars get scattered all across the galaxies.

Initially, the gas and dust in a nebula are spread far apart, but an invisible force called gravity starts pulling them together. It is this force by which planets or other bodies draw objects towards the centre or towards each other.

As these clumps of gas and dust get bigger and bigger, the gravitational force also gets much stronger, and finally, this cloud gets so big that it collapses from its own gravity. This cave-in causes the material at the centre of the cloud to become extremely hot and it begins to glow.

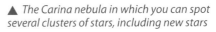

▲ *The Carina nebula in which you can spot several clusters of stars, including new stars*

▲ *Our home galaxy, the Milky Way has millions of stars*

⭐ A Star is Born

A chemical reaction that converts hydrogen into helium takes place in the core of the cloud when the temperature reaches 1,50,00,000° C. This hot centre or core, known as the **protostar,** is the beginning of a new star and is the first step in its evolution. The glowing protostar keeps on accumulating more and more mass, depending on how much matter is available in the nebula. Once the mass has stabilised and it can take no more mass, it is known as a **main sequence star**. At this stage, the star will continue to glow for billions of years.

⭐ The Middle

Just like a car runs out of fuel, a star nearing its end almost runs out of fuel when most of its hydrogen has been converted into helium. This causes the star's core to become unstable and it starts to contract, while the outer shell (consisting mostly of hydrogen) begins to expand. Due to this expansion, the star begins to cool and glows red and becomes a **red giant star.** All stars evolve in the same way until the red giant phase.

▼ *The red giant star is either a low or intermediate mass star*

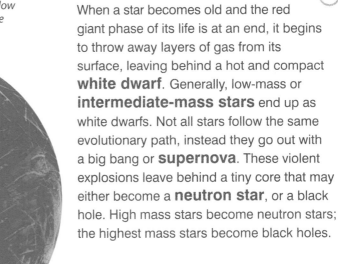

⭐ The End

When a star becomes old and the red giant phase of its life is at an end, it begins to throw away layers of gas from its surface, leaving behind a hot and compact **white dwarf**. Generally, low-mass or **intermediate-mass stars** end up as white dwarfs. Not all stars follow the same evolutionary path, instead they go out with a big bang or **supernova**. These violent explosions leave behind a tiny core that may either become a **neutron star**, or a black hole. High mass stars become neutron stars; the highest mass stars become black holes.

The Life Cycle of Stars

Stars take different paths in their evolutionary cycles. Their life cycles are determined by their mass. We can roughly classify stars into two types—low, intermediate mass stars and high-mass stars. The greater the mass, the shorter the life cycle.

⭐ Main Sequence Stars

Like babies need their food to grow into adults, young stars or protostars develop into main sequence stars by gathering mass from the clouds where they are born. This is the main phase of a star when it actively generates energy. A star can glow and remain in this stage for a few million years to billions of years, depending on its mass and rate of conversion of mass into energy. Generally, very high-mass stars have a faster rate of converting mass into energy and hence they have a shorter lifespan. For example, a very luminous high-mass star in its main phase can burn energy 1000 times faster than the Sun. Its lifespan will be shorter in comparison to a low-mass star.

💡 Isn't It Amazing!

One sugar cube of neutron star material would weigh about 1 trillion kilograms on Earth—almost as much as a mountain!

⭐ Stellar Black Holes

Stellar black holes are created when the core of a really massive dying star (having 20 times the mass of the Sun), collapses upon itself, causing a supernova. A black hole is a place in space where the pull of gravity is so strong (because matter is squeezed into such a minute space) that even light cannot get out. Since light cannot escape, black holes are invisible and cannot be seen directly. They can only be viewed through space telescopes with special tools.

Massive star

Red supergiant

Supernova

Black hole

Neutron star

When the core of a high-mass star collapses, it crushes electrons and protons to form neutrons, creating a neutron star. A neutron star is one of the densest objects that can be viewed directly by astronomers. Imagine an object the size of the Sun pressed into the size of a planet like Earth! Due to this, the gravitation on its surface is tremendous. A neutron star also has a very powerful magnetic field.

▼ *A neutron star in space*

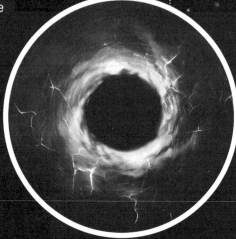

▲ *A black hole in space*

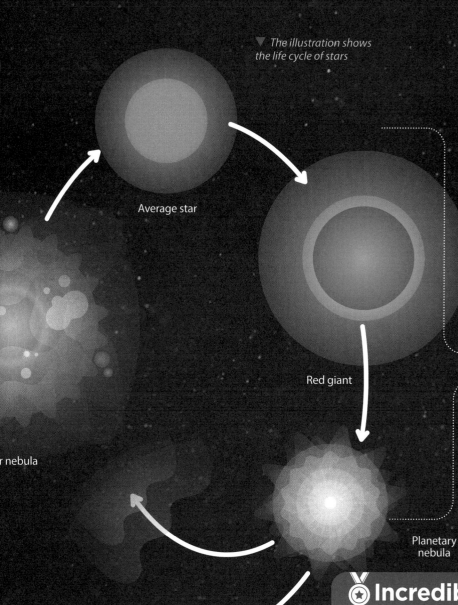

▼ *The illustration shows the life cycle of stars*

Average star

Red giant

Planetary nebula

White dwarf

nebula

As a star continues to glow and hydrogen is converted into helium at its core through nuclear fusion, the centre becomes unstable and starts to contract. The outer layer of the star (still mostly hydrogen), begins to expand. When this expansion happens, the star reaches the red giant phase, i.e. it cools and starts to glow red. It is red since it is cooler than the protostar and it is a giant because its outer shell has expanded outward. Almost all stars evolve the same way up to the red giant stage.

▲ *The burning atmosphere of a red giant star*

When all the hydrogen gas contained in the outer shell of a star blows away, it forms a ring around the core or centre and is called a planetary nebula.

▲ *An image of a planetary nebula*

In the case of stars like the Sun, when only the hot stellar core is left behind and the outer layers have all gone, the burning and dense core is called a white dwarf star. This is the fate of only those stars with a mass up to 1.4 times the mass of the Sun. Did you know that the Sun will become a white dwarf billions of years later?

▲ *A white dwarf star*

⭐ Incredible Individuals

Stephen Hawking (1942–2018) was a much-admired English theoretical physicist of the late 20th and early 21st century. His best-selling book published in 1988 (also a motion picture)—*A Brief History of Time: From the Big Bang to Black Holes*—made him a celebrity. Hawking's main work revolved around the study of black holes, the remains from the collapse of giant stars. He also worked in the areas of general relativity, thermodynamics and quantum mechanics in his attempt to understand how the universe was formed.

His achievements are all the more praiseworthy due to his battle with a degenerative muscular disease, which damaged his nerves and muscle system. The illness left him without the ability to write and he could barely speak. It forced him to be confined to a motorised wheelchair. Despite these setbacks, Hawking continued to pursue his pioneering work in the field of astronomy and popularised the subject.

▶ *Stephen Hawking*

Nebulas: The Birthplace of Stars

Stars are born within nebulas found in interstellar space (region between stars). Astronomers have studied different nebulas in the Milky Way galaxy using powerful telescopes. They look like beautiful, delicate paintings with a vibrant array of colours.

▼ *The cloud associated with the Rosette nebula, a stellar nursery about 5,000 light years away from Earth*

⭐ What is a Nebula?

A nebula is a giant cloud of gas (hydrogen and helium) and dust from which stars are born. No two nebulas look the same. They differ in appearance due to variations in temperature and density of the material observed. They also differ depending on how the material is situated in space in relation to the observer.

Nebulas are often referred to as 'star nurseries' because they are regions where a new star starts to develop. Other nebulas are formed from the gas and dust which is generated when a star dies in a massive explosion known as a supernova.

Based on their appearance, nebulas are classified into dark nebulas and bright nebulas. The dark ones are irregularly shaped black patches in the sky and block out the light of the stars that lie beyond. The bright nebulas are fairly luminous, glowing surfaces either emitting their own light or reflecting light from nearby stars.

👤 In Real Life

Celestial photography or astrophotography is an interesting hobby or career that one can pursue. It involves clicking photographs of objects in space, like stars, planets, comets, galaxies and also events like eclipses, etc. Beautiful landscapes of the magnificent night sky can be captured on camera when it is less polluted. Many photographs which we get to see of the Milky Way and of star trails are taken by astrophotographers. Often, photographs clicked by astrophotographers give us an artistic view of the night sky and are such visual treats that they help generate excitement and interest in astronomy and the universe.

The Veil Nebula

National Aeronautics and Space Administration's Hubble Space Telescope discovered the Veil nebula, an exquisite remnant of one of the best-known supernovas caused by the explosion of a massive star 20 times bigger than the Sun. The star exploded nearly 8,000 years ago. The nebula gets its name from its elegant and beautiful structure and resides in the constellation of Cygnus, the Swan, about 2,100 light years away.

The Orion Nebula

One of the earliest observed nebulas was the Orion nebula, located in the sword of the hunter's figure in the constellation of Orion. The nebula was discovered in 1610, two years after the invention of the telescope, by French scholar Nicolas-Claude Fabri de Peiresc. It was the first nebula to be photographed in 1880 by Henry Draper in US. The Orion Nebula is 1,350 light years away from Earth and contains hundreds of very hot young stars clustered around four massive stars known as the Trapezium.

▼ The Veil Nebula

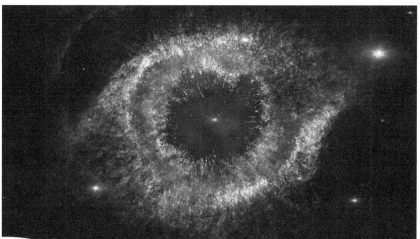

▲ The Helix nebula

▲ The Orion nebula

The Helix Nebula

The Helix nebula is the closest to Earth and the largest known planetary nebula which is located in the constellation of Aquarius. It is 700 light years away, so it would take a human being travelling at the speed of light 700 years to reach there!

The Crab Nebula

In 1,054 CE, Chinese and other astronomers first observed the Crab nebula. It gets its name from the fact that its shape resembles a crab and it is filled with mysterious, thin thread-like structures. This nebula is about 10 light years away.

◀ The Palomar Observatory in California

What's a Supernova?

High-mass stars die in a huge explosion called a supernova and finally end up either as neutron stars or as black holes. Supernovas are extremely important for scientists to study because they tell us more about how the universe was formed.

Another Star Bites the Dust

Supernovas are a class of violently exploding stars whose luminosity, after eruption, suddenly increases several million times its normal level. The term supernova comes from nova (meaning 'new' in Latin). Supernovas are characterised by a tremendous, rapid brightening which lasts for a few weeks, and then slowly dims down. A supernova explosion is catastrophic for a star and ends its active or energy-generating life. Massive amounts of matter, equal to the material of several Suns, may get blown into space when a star 'goes supernova'.

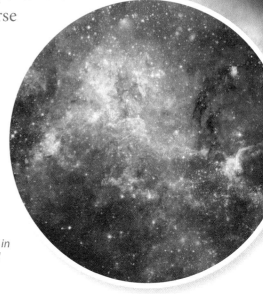

 ▶ *A supernova explosion with glowing nebula in the background*

Supernova of a Single Star

There are two types of supernova. One occurs at the end of a single star's lifetime, when the star begins to cool down and runs out of its nuclear fuel, resulting in some of its mass flowing into its core, or in other words, the force of gravity takes over. The star cannot withstand its own gravitational force and collapses. This cave-in happens in a matter of 15 seconds and is so fast that it causes tremendous shock waves and causes the outer part of the star to explode, leaving behind a dense core and an expanding cloud of dust and gas. If the star is a supergiant, its supernova can also create and leave behind the densest object in the universe—a black hole.

◀ *Stellar mass black hole*

Supernova of a Binary Star System

Another type of supernova takes place in a binary system of stars when two stars orbit the same point and at least one of those stars is a white dwarf. If one white dwarf strikes against the other or if one of them sucks out or gobbles up too much matter from the nearby star, the white dwarf will explode, causing a supernova.

It is easier to spot and see supernovas in other galaxies rather than in our own Milky Way galaxy, since dust obstructs our view.

◀ *An illustration showing a white dwarf pulling matter from a companion star*

Incredible Individuals

In August 2018, NASA awarded its highest honour, the Distinguished Public Service Medal, to astronomer Yervant Terzian. He was honoured with this recognition for his dedicated contribution and impact on education, public service and scientific research. He has played a huge role in inspiring young students as well as the public at large.

Much to his credit, Terzian has been part of eight NASA committees, including the Hubble Space Telescope Fellowship Committee. He is famous for his studies of stellar evolution and the discovery of regions of hydrogen gas between galaxies. This discovery indicated the presence of unseen matter in intergalactic space. He has authored and co-authored over 235 scientific publications!

▲ *A binary star system with a red dwarf and a blue giant*

⭐ Star Dust

Supernovas can lead us to a lot of important information. Supernovas involving white dwarfs are used to measure distances in space. Another lesson is that stars are like factories of the universe, manufacturing vital chemicals within their cores like carbon, nitrogen, and oxygen—all life-forming elements that make up our universe.

Massive stars create elements like gold, silver, uranium and platinum, which also aid the universe in creating generations of stars, planets, etc. Human beings carry some remains of these explosions in their bodies. In fact, everything in the universe is created from scattered star dust!

⭐ Studying Supernovas

Scientists at NASA use different types of telescopes to study supernovas. For example, the NuSTAR (Nuclear Spectroscopic Telescope Array) mission, uses X-ray vision to investigate the universe.

◀ *A visual representation of the NuSTAR (Nuclear Spectroscopic Telescope Array)*

💡 Isn't It Amazing!

Supernovas cast off or eject matter into space at a speed of 15,000 to 40,000 kilometres per second.

Homeless Stars

Galaxies are home to the stars. Intergalactic (situated in or relating to the spaces between galaxies) stars do not have a home in a galaxy, although at one time they may have belonged to one. Some of these stars display unusual traits which make them stand out from the rest. Yet others streak across space at tremendous speeds.

 ## What are Intergalactic Stars?

Rogue stars are created due to galaxy interactions and mergers which take place in the early phase of a galaxy cluster. During such interactions, stars are torn away from their home galaxies and thrown into intergalactic space, where they roam free from the gravitational pull of a galaxy.

Astronomers were able to learn more about these rogue stars by observing their motion and the motion of nearby galaxies. The motion of such rogue stars is governed by the gravitational field of the entire cluster, rather than the pull of any one galaxy. Therefore, scientists concluded that these stars are in between galaxies or 'intergalactic'.

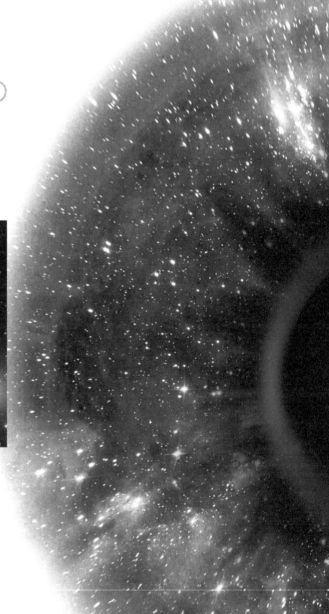

▼ *Stars getting sucked into a black hole due to the extreme pull of its gravity*

 ## Outcast Stars

The Virgo cluster is the closest large cluster of galaxies. It is so huge that it contains over 2,000 galaxies! With the help of NASA's Hubble Space Telescope, scientists have so far discovered 600 such outcast stars in the Virgo cluster, which is 60 million light years from Earth. All of them are bright red giants.

▲ *Virgo cluster of galaxies*

💡 Isn't It Amazing!

Despite travelling at hypervelocities, it would take a star about 10 million years to travel from the centre to the spiral's edge, 50,000 light years away!

Speedy Gonzales

A **hypervelocity** (extremely high speed) star is one which is kicked out from its galaxy at a very high speed. Although it is not at all easy for a star to be ejected from its home, this happens when it gets extremely close to a supermassive black hole. This black hole lies in the centre of the galaxy. The star hurtles out with such force and travels at such high speeds that it escapes from the clutches of its galaxy's gravity.

In 2005, astronomers discovered the very first hypervelocity star. Much later, 16 other such hypervelocity stars were identified. In 2012, astronomers reported a group of more than 675 such rogue stars found on the periphery of the Milky Way galaxy. They claim these are hypervelocity stars which have been thrown out from the galactic core. These particular stars were selected by them due to their unusual red colour and their location in intergalactic space between the Milky Way galaxy and the Andromeda galaxy.

▲ *The bright spot on the top-left is the hypervelocity star. Credit: ESA/Hubble, NASA, S. Geier*

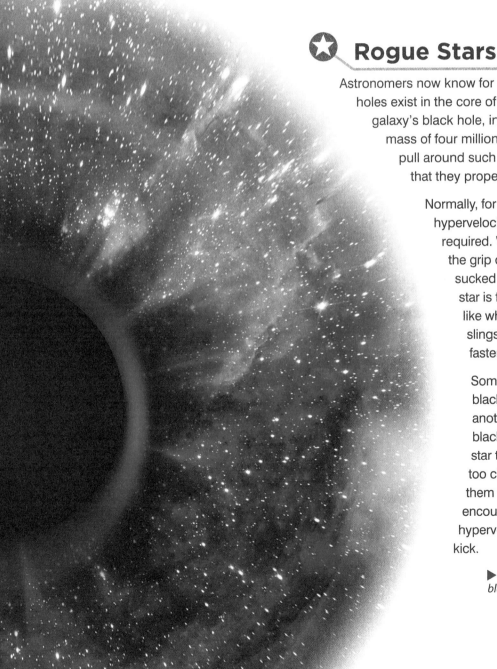

Rogue Stars

Astronomers now know for a fact that very big black holes exist in the core of many galaxies. The Milky Way galaxy's black hole, in fact, is estimated to have a mass of four million solar masses. The gravitational pull around such huge black holes is so strong that they propel stars to such hypervelocities.

Normally, for stars to go 'rogue' or attain hypervelocity, a binary pair of stars is required. When the pair gets entangled in the grip of the black hole, one star gets sucked in, while the other companion star is flung out at great speed—much like what happens to a stone in a slingshot, but at a much, much faster speed.

Sometimes, a central black hole eats up another smaller black hole. Any star that comes too close to them then will encounter a hypervelocity kick.

▶ *A supermassive black hole*

Starry Facts

Is the Sun the most important star in the universe? How does it compare with other stars? Almost all the stars that you see in the dark night sky are bigger and brighter than the Sun. A few of the faint ones are about the same size and brightness.

⭐ Sunshine

The star nearest to us is the Sun. The next closest star to Earth is nearly 2,50,000 times farther away. For us on Earth and for the solar system, it is the most important object. The Sun provides us with life-giving light, heat and energy.

⭐ How Big are Stars?

Although the Sun is impressive, compared to the billions of other stars in the universe, it is not as special. The largest of stars may be as much as 3,21,86,88,000 kilometres away. If such a huge star were in the centre of our solar system, it would perhaps gobble up all the planets, including Earth! In comparison, the Sun is about 13,92,000 kilometres in diameter. This makes the Sun 109 times wider than Earth. Yet, it is an average-sized star in the universe.

▶ *The Sun compared to other stars*

Sun   Aldebaran   Rigel   Antares

Far, Far and Away

How far are the Sun and the other stars from Earth? They are very, very, very far away… much farther than you can ever imagine! The Sun, which is the closest to us, is 150 million kilometres from Earth. All the other stars are much farther away!

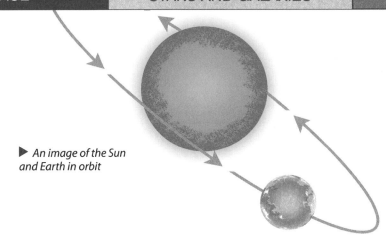

▶ *An image of the Sun and Earth in orbit*

Hottest Objects

Stars are amongst the hottest objects found in space. The hottest stars can be almost 55,538° C. This big number shows us that stars are much hotter than anything we will ever experience on Earth. The Sun is about 5,538° C. So, in comparison to the hottest stars, it is much cooler, but still very, very hot. Much hotter than the temperature in an oven! And these temperatures are only at the surface. The cores of stars are even hotter. The mindboggling large numbers above give you an idea of how extremely hot stars like the Sun can get. Can you imagine what would happen if people got too close to the Sun?

The heat from a star also impacts the planets orbiting it. The closer the planets orbit near a star, the hotter they will be. In the case of our solar system, for example, Mercury and Venus are closer to the Sun than Earth, and are, therefore, much warmer than Earth. On the other hand, Earth is closer to the Sun than Mars and hence warmer than Mars. If a planet is too hot, all the water on it will evaporate. Imagine if that were the case on Earth, how would we live without water? If the planet is too far, it would be too cold to sustain life. Are we not lucky to be living on a lovely planet which is at just the right distance from the Sun? It keeps us warm and yet not too hot!

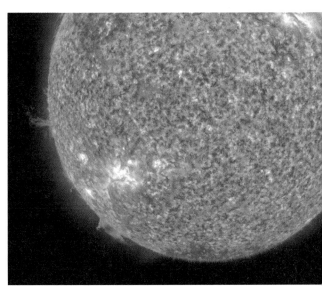

▲ *The Sun photographed by NASA's Solar Dynamics Observatory*

▲ *Betelgeuse*

 Isn't It Amazing!

If you were to visit the Sun and drive all the way around it in a car at a speed of about 97 kilometres per hour, without a break, it would take you five years to get there!

Stories from the Andromeda and Milky Way

The Andromeda galaxy has a special significance in relation to the Milky Way galaxy. Not only is it a large and major galaxy closest to the Milky Way, but it is also colliding with it. Stars in the Andromeda galaxy can be seen with the naked eye on moonless nights, and it is richly populated with them.

▲ *The largest image of the Andromeda galaxy taken by the Hubble Telescope. Credit: NASA, ESA, J. Dalcanton (University of Washington, USA), B. F. Williams (University of Washington, USA), L. C. Johnson (University of Washington, USA), the PHAT team, and R. Gendler*

★ Star-packed Andromeda

Scientists have found densely packed stars in the innermost core of the galaxy. The outer disc was found to have far fewer stars. A majority of the stars in the centre of the galaxy are the cooler yellow ones (lower left side in the picture above). The outer blue, ring-like formation which extends from top-left to the bottom-right is the spiral arm of the Andromeda galaxy. It comprises numerous clusters of young, blue stars and star-forming regions. In January 2015, NASA's Hubble Telescope revealed that Andromeda has 100 million stars and thousands of star clusters!

★ The Milky Way-Andromeda Collision

Scientists have found that the Milky Way galaxy and the Andromeda galaxy are colliding and moving towards each other at a very high speed. But this will not happen during our lives. The two galaxies will merge only four billion years from now, but stars from Andromeda will not hit us on our planet. We are told that the stars are very far apart from each other and will merely go past. Since galaxies are also made up of gas and dust, when the clouds collide with one another, they will create new stars.

◀ *The Andromeda galaxy against our galaxy, the Milky Way*

⊛ Incredible Individuals

Edwin Hubble (1889–1953) studied law only to please his father, who insisted upon it. After his father died in 1913, he followed his passion and studied astronomy in Chicago. He also served in the US army during both World Wars. Between 1923–1925, he was responsible for identifying a particular class of stars (Cepheid variables) in three nebulas and definitively proving that these were outside the Milky Way galaxy. This demonstrated that our galaxy is not the universe and that other galaxies exist outside the Milky Way. Hubble's study of galaxies also helped in developing a standard classification system of elliptical, spiral and irregular galaxies which are spread out evenly at great distances. NASA's well-known Hubble Space Telescope is named after him.

◀ *Edwin Hubble*

Ancient Ideas and Uses of Stars

Have you ever looked up at the sky and felt a sense of wonder mixed with curiosity about the Sun, the stars and the universe? You are not alone. For centuries, human beings have looked to the skies with a sense of mystery. Our ancestors used stars and **constellations** for several different reasons throughout history.

Stars and Religion

Probably the very first use and ideas revolving around stars and constellations were religious. People thought that the Gods lived in the heavens and so, they must be responsible for making them.

Several cultures believed that the position of the stars was one way for God to tell them stories. Therefore, they started imagining shapes and giving names to star groups and telling stories about them. Most of our constellation names are derived from Greek culture and are named after mythological Greek heroes and legends. Different cultures gave different meanings to the same constellations.

▲ Ancient people looked to the Sun, stars and planets for religious purposes, to foretell seasons, and for navigation

💡 Isn't It Amazing!

Did you know that when you look out into space, you are actually looking back in time? This is because light emitted by very far-off objects, like stars and galaxies, takes a long time to reach us. By the time it does, we are actually seeing what the objects looked like a while ago and not what they look like in real time.

Stars helped in Navigation

Long before radio navigation, radar and global positioning system (GPS) technologies were invented, early seamen or mariners sailed using the Sun and the stars to guide them. Polynesians were able to sail across thousands of miles in the Pacific Ocean using their knowledge of stars and constellations. Ancient Minoans who lived on the Mediterranean island of Crete did the same. Polaris (the North Star) was often used to navigate since it was easy to locate in the Little Dipper constellation.

Stars and Agriculture

Early men used stars and constellations to decide what was the best time for sowing and harvesting. Constellations helped them gain information about each season. For example, they knew that when the Orion constellation was completely visible, it was time for winter.

Polaris (North Star)

Ursa Minor (Little Dipper)

Ursa Major (Big Dipper)

▲ The Polaris or North Star helped early seafarers to navigate

Stargazers

The theories about the laws of nature and how celestial bodies exist and function are numerous and as vast as our universe. Over centuries, with improvements in technology and the invention of sophisticated equipment like powerful space telescopes, better cameras, etc., more accurate studies have been possible than in the early days before such equipment was invented.

 1546–1601

 1730–1817

 1738–1822

Tycho Brahe

Brahe was a Danish astronomer known for developing astronomical instruments and measuring and fixing the accurate positions of 777 stars.

1572: His discovery of a 'new star' brighter than Venus led him to upturn the then prevalent theory of inner and continuous harmony of the whole world. This harmony was ruled by the stars, which were thought to be perfect and unchanging. Brahe's study of the dramatic changes in stars challenged this age-old law.

1573: He published his observations of the new star in *De Nova Stella*.

Charles Messier

He was a French astronomer who worked under Joseph-Nicolas Delisle, another noted French astronomer.

1758–1759: He was the first to spot the Halley's Comet and thus began his passion to look for new comets. He was responsible for locating 13 comets.

1760: He made a list of nebulas to help differentiate them from comets. Many of them are referred to by using his catalogue system. He was the first to compile such a catalogue.

Sir William Herschel

Herschel was a German-born British astronomer and composer.

1781: He became famous for his discovery of the planet Uranus—the first planet to be located since prehistoric times.

1784–1785: He first suggested that nebulas are composed of stars and developed the theory of stellar evolution.

Edward Emerson Barnard

Barnard was a leading American astronomer of his time and a pioneer in celestial photography.

1889: He started photographing the Milky Way with a more technologically advanced camera, which helped reveal new data.

1892: He discovered 16 comets and Jupiter's fifth satellite.

1916: He discovered the star (Barnard's Star) that has the greatest known **proper motion** (motion of an individual star relative to other stars).

1919: He published a catalogue on dark nebulas.

Hans Albrecht Bethe

Bethe was a German-born American theoretical physicist who helped shape quantum physics.

1938: He studied and provided conclusive answers to the problem of energy generation in stars and explained how stars could burn for billions of years by specifying and analysing the nuclear reactions responsible for this.

1967: He was awarded the Nobel Prize based on his 1939 paper on energy generation in stars which helped create the field of nuclear **astrophysics**.

 1857–1923 **1900–1979** **1906–2005**  **1910–1995**

Cecilia Payne-Gaposchkin

Cecilia was a British-born American astronomer who discovered that stars are mainly made of hydrogen and helium. She also established that stars could be classified according to their temperatures.

1925: She published a thesis on stellar atmospheres.

1930: She studied the luminosity of stars and published a book titled *Stars of High Luminosity*.

Subrahmanyan Chandrasekhar

1931: Chandrasekhar said that a star with mass more than 1.44 times that of the Sun does not, in fact, form a white dwarf. Instead, it continues to collapse, blowing off its gaseous covering in a supernova explosion and becoming a neutron star. An even bigger star continues to collapse and becomes a black hole. His calculations contributed to our understanding of supernovas, neutron stars and black holes.

1983: He won the Nobel Prize in Physics for his theories on the evolution of stars.

Modern Star Discoveries

The study and science of astronomy is vast and never-ending. Every day, there are new discoveries being unravelled by scientists around the world. Here are some which will amaze you!

⭐ Silica Remnants Detected in Distant Supernovas

The next time you pick up a glass of water or walk down a road, remember that the materials used to make them were incubated billions of years ago by exploding stars!

Observations made by NASA's Spitzer Space Telescope have helped a new study reveal that silica—a key ingredient in sand and glass—is formed when massive stars explode in a supernova. 60 per cent of Earth's crust is made of it. Besides in the manufacture of glass and sand-and-gravel mixtures for construction, silica has numerous other uses.

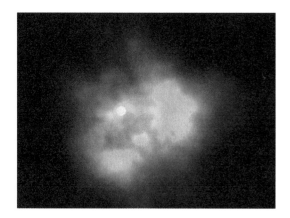

◀ *This image of the supernova remnant (G54.1+0.3) includes radio, infrared and X-ray light*

⭐ The Farthest Star Ever Spotted

Thanks to a rare and peculiar natural phenomenon that helped greatly magnify (by approximately 600 times) the star's feeble glow, astronomers were able to discover the farthest star ever seen. Helped by NASA's Hubble Space Telescope, the star (nicknamed Icarus) is located more than halfway across the universe. If not for this quirk of nature, this gigantic blue star would have been too faint to detect even with the world's largest telescopes. This discovery made in April 2018 has paved a new path for astronomers to study individual stars in far-off galaxies.

▼ *A magnificent and glittering ball of stars lies in the centre of the Large Magellanic Cloud. Source: ESA/Hubble*

⭐ Star Cluster Spied in Nearby Galaxy

A gorgeous, diamond-studded cluster of stars was captured on camera in October 2018 by NASA's Hubble advanced-technology cameras. This globular cluster lies towards the centre of the Large Magellanic Cloud, a dwarf galaxy and one of Earth's closest neighbours. The galaxy is richly populated with numerous star clusters, making it an astronomer's dream lab for studying star formation. This cluster was first discovered in November 1834 by British astronomer John Herschel and has been studied extensively since then.

⭐ Mystery of Exploding Stars Solved

Scientists have now been able to solve the puzzle of what causes exploding stars which are used to measure the fast-paced expansion of the universe. An international study at the Australian National University (ANU) observed a small-sized star hurtling through our galaxy at breakneck speed. They concluded this star to be a fragment from a massive explosion that took place millions of years ago.

The supernova explosion took place in a binary system, where a super-dense white dwarf had run out of fuel and sucked mass from its giant star companion. The mass it gathered created a chemical reaction, causing a star piece to run away. The violent explosion also resulted in the destruction of the binary system. This runaway star caught the attention of scientists because it was hurtling around in the galaxy at extremely fast speeds and seemed to have an unusual chemical composition.

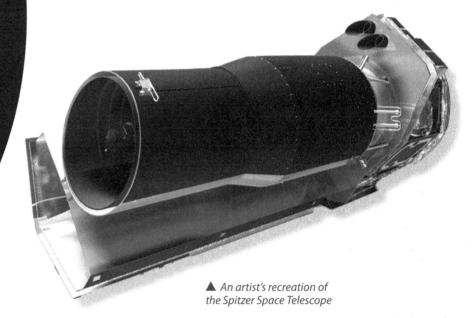

▲ An artist's recreation of the Spitzer Space Telescope

◀ Supernova explosion of a white dwarf star around a giant red star

⭐ Sub-Saturn like Planet Discovered around a Sun-like Star

The Indian Space Research Organisation (ISRO) discovered a sub-Saturn or super-Neptune sized planet having a mass of approximately 27 times that of Earth and a radii six times bigger, orbiting a Sun-like star. Till date, only 23 such planetary systems (including this one) are known. This discovery is crucial to understanding how such super-Neptune or sub-Saturn kind of planets, which are too close to the host star, are formed, as well as how planet-formations occur around Sun-like stars. With this study, India became one of the few countries which have managed to discover a planet around a star beyond the solar system. The apparatus used to make this discovery and to measure the mass of a planet with such precise measurements was designed in-house and is the first of its kind in Asia.

The Lucky Ones

An infinite number of stars exist within our universe. Some of them are better known than others because they are more easily visible with the unaided eye and are perhaps the brightest objects in the celestial sky. Most of them will, therefore, also have been observed and studied for many years. Which are some of these lucky stars that have received so much attention and left human beings star-struck?

▲ *The Guiding Star or Polaris*

★ Polaris

Polaris is the present North Star. Earth spins around its axis. If you follow this imaginary line from the northern pole, it would point to a particular star, which is the Polaris and therefore referred to as the North Star. Since it is close to the North Pole, this star has been used as a tool for navigation in the northern hemisphere and is also known as the Guiding Star. Due to the wobbling of Earth's axis, in about another 14,000 years, it will slowly start pointing away from the Polaris towards a new North Star!

▲ *Alpha Centauri is a very bright yellowish star in the constellation of Centaurus*

★ Alpha Centauri

The Alpha Centauri is a triple star system and is the closest to the Sun. It consists of Proxima Centauri (its dimmest component) and its brighter components— Alpha Centauri A and B. When seen from Earth, it is the fourth brightest star after Sirius, Canopus and Arcturus. It lies in the southern constellation Centaurus. Alpha Centauri was designated as Rigil Kentaurus by the IAU in 2016; the word is of Arabic origin and means 'foot of the Centaur'.

▲ *Betelgeuse is one of the largest stars currently known. Credit: ALMA (ESO/ NAOJ/NRAO)/E. O'Gorman/P. Kervella*

★ Betelgeuse

Betelgeuse is one of the most luminous stars seen at night and the second-brightest in the Orion constellation. It is a red supergiant and it sure is humungous, being nearly 950 times larger than the Sun! Its name comes from the Arabic word 'bat al-jawz', which means 'giant's shoulder'. Betelgeuse can be easily spotted due to its position in Orion and its deep red hue.

▲ *Sirius or the Dog Star—the brightest star seen from Earth. Credit: NASA, ESA, H. Bond (STScI), and M. Barstow (University of Leicester)*

★ Sirius

Sirius is significant in more ways than one, firstly it is the brightest star amongst all other stars seen from Earth. Ancient Egyptians called it Sothis and believed it to be the cause of the Nile floods, which always seemed to coincide with the first rising of Sirius in the year. It is a binary star in the constellation Canis Major. It has a radius 1.71 times that of the Sun. Sirius means 'sparkling' or 'scorching' in Greek.

▲ *Vega, as seen by NASA's Spitzer Space Telescope*

★ Vega

Vega is the fifth-brightest in the night sky and the brightest star in the northern constellation, Lyra. It is located at a distance of approximately 25 light years, which makes it one of the Sun's closer neighbours. Vega is surrounded by a sphere of dust similar to the solar system's **Kuiper Belt**. Its claim to fame one day in the future will be that it will become the next North Star by 14,000 CE.

▲ *Rigel and the Witch Head nebula*

★ Rigel

Rigel is one of the brightest bluish-white supergiants in the Orion constellation. Its distance from the Sun is about 870 light years and it is 47,000 times more luminous than the Sun.

What's in a Name?

Stars have been named and catalogued since prehistoric times. The naming and cataloguing of stars plays an important role in the science of astronomy. It helps scientists and enthusiastic stargazers to accurately locate stars from anywhere on Earth. There has also been a tradition in both the scientific world and the general public to pay tribute to a person by naming a star after them.

▶ *The book written by Bayer catalogued stars visible to the naked eye*

 ## History of Star Catalogues

For centuries, various cultures and civilisations all over the world have labelled and given names to the stars in the night sky. Many of these names have their origin in Greek, Latin and Arabic cultures. Some of these names are in use even today. With the development of astronomy over the years, there was a need felt to have a universal cataloguing system, whereby the most-studied and brightest stars were referred to by the same labels, regardless of the country or culture from where the astronomers came.

The earliest known 'cataloguing system' which is still popular today, was created by Johann Bayer in 1603, in his book *Uranometria*, a star atlas. He used lowercase Greek letters to label stars in each constellation roughly in the order of their observable brightness. So, according to this labelling system, the brightest star was generally labelled Alpha (though not always) and the second brightest was Beta and so forth. For example, the brightest star in Cygnus (the Swan) is Alpha Cygni. However, this cataloguing system ran into problems—the Greek alphabet had only 24 letters and was not enough to name the thousands of stars found in constellations; often due to inaccurate estimates and other irregularities, this system did not always work precisely.

Nearly 200 years later, English astronomer John Flamsteed started another naming scheme. From his observations at Greenwich, Flamsteed made the first main star catalogue (published in 1725, after his death) with the help of a telescope. The Flamsteed numbers as we know them now, however, were not assigned by him but by a French astronomer, Jerome Lalande in his French version of Flamsteed's catalogue published in 1783.

◀ *John Flamsteed*

Incredible Individuals

Edward Barnard (1889–1953) began his career as a poor photographer. Much to his credit, he later became a well-known astronomer. He made his own telescope and discovered several comets. He went on to discover Amalthea, the fifth known moon of Jupiter. He studied the physical features of planets, comets, nebulas and novas. One of his most important contributions was the introduction of wide-field photographic methods to study the Milky Way. He also discovered, amongst other things, the star with the largest known proper motion, which has been named Barnard's Star after him.

▶ The arrow points to Barnard's Star

⭐ The Christening of Stars

To promote and safeguard all aspects of astronomy including research, communication, education and development through international cooperation, an organisation was founded in 1919 known as the International Astronomical Union (IAU). IAU consists of individual members (professionals working in this field) and national members, i.e. 82 countries that are its members. IAU is the internationally recognised authority for naming and giving designations and surface features to celestial bodies.

Very few stars which have cultural, historical and astrophysical importance have proper names (e.g. Vega, Polaris, Betelgeuse). In the professional community, however, stars are assigned designations which are alphanumerical (e.g. HR 7001)—this makes it easier to locate, describe and discuss them.

▼ An illustration of the Merz and Mahler refracting telescope at the Cincinnati Observatory in Ohio, USA

These alphanumerical designations are usually sorted by the position of the star. This system has made it much easier to look them up in catalogues. Accurate positions found via catalogue numbers help facilitate precise identification and are beneficial especially while cataloguing stars since there are billions and trillions of them.

In fact, stars did not have 'official' names until 2016, which is when the IAU approved 227 common names for stars. Another 86 names drawn from other cultures like Australian Aboriginal, Hindu, Chinese, Mayan, South African and a few others were added to this list in 2017.

💡 Isn't It Amazing!

The Ara constellation has a star known as Cervantes named after the Spanish author Miguel de Cervantes who wrote the famous novel *Don Quixote*.

Word Check

Astrophysics: It is a branch of astronomy concerned primarily with the properties and structures of cosmic objects, including the universe as a whole.

Binary system: It refers to two stars bound together by gravitational forces and orbiting around a common centre of mass.

Black hole: A huge amount of matter packed into a small area that results in a gravitational field that is so strong that nothing, not even light, can escape from it

Constellation: In astronomy, it refers to any certain groupings of stars that were imagined to form conspicuous configurations of objects or creatures in the sky

Convection: It is a process by which heat is transferred by movement of a heated fluid such as air or water.

Globular cluster: They are large groups of old stars that are closely packed in a symmetrical, somewhat spherical form.

High-mass star: It is a star that is three times the mass of the Sun.

Hypervelocity: It refers to extremely high velocity or speed. Velocity is the speed at which something moves in a particular direction.

Intergalactic: It means to be situated in or relating to the spaces between galaxies or relating to or occurring in outer space.

Intermediate-mass star: It is a star with a lifespan of between 50 million and 20 billion years.

Kuiper Belt: It is a flat ring of icy small bodies that revolve around the Sun, beyond the orbit of the planet Neptune.

Light year: In astronomy, the distance that light travels in one year is called a light year.

Low-mass star: It is a star with a mass that is less than half the mass of the Sun.

Luminosity: It is the amount of light emitted by an object in a unit of time.

Main sequence stars: Like the Sun, these exist in a state of nuclear fusion during which they emit energy for billions of years by converting hydrogen to helium.

Nebula: It is a cloud of gas and dust in which a star is generally born.

Neutron star: It can form after the core of a high-mass star collapses. The impact crushes the protons and electrons into densely packed neutrons.

Nuclear fusion: It is a process by which nuclear reactions between light elements form heavier elements.

Open cluster: In astronomy, it is any group of young stars held together by mutual gravitation.

Proper motion: It is the motion of an individual star relative to other stars.

Protostar: It is the beginning of a new star and is the first step in the star's evolution.

Radiation: It is a flow of atomic and subatomic particles and of waves, such as those that characterise heat rays, light rays and X-rays.

Red giant star: It is a star that is larger than the Sun and red because it has a lower temperature.

Self-luminous: It refers to a body having, in itself, the property of emitting light.

Stellar classification: It is a scheme for assigning stars to types according to their temperatures, as estimated from their spectra.

Supernova: A massive stellar explosion resulting in a brief increase in luminosity and the ejection of matter

White dwarf star: It is a small star, about the size of Earth. It is one of the last stages of a star's life.